WHILE I YET LIVE

Gboyega Odubanjo is a British-Nigerian poet born and raised in East London. In 2018 he completed an MA in Poetry at the University of East Anglia. Gboyega was published in Bad Betty Press anthology, *The Dizziness of Freedom*, and is a member of the Barbican Young Poets, the Roundhouse Poetry Collective, and (In)Space.

While I Yet Live

Published by Bad Betty Press in 2019
www.badbettypress.com

All rights reserved

The right of Gboyega Odubanjo to be identified as the author of this work has been asserted by him in accordance with Section 77 of the Copyright, Designs and Patents Act of 1988.

Cover design by Amy Acre

Printed and bound in the United Kingdom

A CIP record of this book is available from the British Library.

ISBN: 978-1-9997147-6-5

WHILE I YET LIVE
GBOYEGA ODUBANJO

BAD BETTY PRESS

I have death in my pouch.

– Fela Kuti

While I Yet Live

With thanks to my family, friends, and teachers.

Contents

OBIT.	11
White Bronco	12
I	14
Poems (With Drums)	15
Money Dance	17
If I Could Travel to Any Place and Any Time I Would	18
Watershed	19
Ineffable Name	20
Holy Roller	22
We	24
JOHN 19:28	25
Confessions in 3/4 Timing	26
Songs in the Key of Terror	27
Swimming	29
Notes	30

OBIT.
After César Vallejo

i will die in london in the neighbourhood
i grew up in outside the town hall
on the high street. i will have been stabbed
and my killer will look just like me so
no-one will look for him. my body
will remain dead in daylight for hours until
the sky turns more blick than blue. on the news
i will be smiling. i will be as handsome
as i have ever been. today a young man
has died they will say today a young man has died today
it will be a friday a young man has died young o so terribly
young. i will die again three days later
when i hand myself in no-one will believe it because
i will look just like me. i will look like i have died o so
many times already. i will be survived by myself
and the many times that i still have to die.

White Bronco

sat on something expensive   seatbelt holding everything
remind you to drive slow so we can keep the windows down   slow
so sun don't blur into moon so the streetlights

don't come before we're ready   if i'm right then we've still got at
least a couple songs left in the tank   i know very little about cars
but i know enough to know i probably look really cool

when i let my arm hang out the passenger side   i smoke
but do not inhale   i know everybody's watching now
watching as we drive slow

slow across the tarmac now   know we could go wherever now
take me to the park   to the river   to my mother's house
promise me you'll drive slow   started driving

so long ago   we could forget where we came from if we wanted to
no   i want you to know exactly where i came from   tell me
they'll keep watching

'til we get to where we're going   tell me that you'll drive slow
still driving   and it's darker now   lights been chasing us
a long time

my mother she's been calling me
i pray that you drive slower now   tell my mother i won't be
coming home

tell me that you'll drive slow   i want you to never stop   never
stop driving now
i want you   never stop   tell me that

I[1]

        look ahead   filled   foreboding [

You]   like   roman   see   river

                                    foaming

intractable   coming

    all but come

---

1   after Enoch Powell

Poems (With Drums)

on my birthday my aunties bring me gold, frankincense and shea butter

i want to write a poem and i want everyone to like it

i don't want to stop until i've got all of the black out of my greys

a friend told me that the problem with birthdays is that you are forced to think about yourself in the third person and most people don't care

it is all noise

here, i imagine light drums in the background

in this poem a loved one is almost dead and we are all in their living room watching a recording from their 50th birthday and they are dancing and i don't know what it is like to look upon oneself and be so removed

in this poem a stranger on a train tells me to get out of this country the first chance i get

in an earlier poem i am a boat and you are an ocean

[more drums]

not understanding a prayer is no reason not to say amen

it's just noise

i remember being told that if i needed to write about love then i never needed to actually say love

i don't think that i ever need to actually fall in love because i have already watched all of the sitcoms and the actors have already done the loving for me

i think all that i need is to start talking and to never stop

it will all just be noise

[drums, louder now]

in this poem, maybe it needs

[more drums, more drums]

i want to write a poem that is partially muted on primetime television that is a group of young men dressed in black dancing aggressively on stage that is nothing but a mouth of chicken and hennessy trading substance for melody my mother said boy i pray you don't embarrass me i want to write about disillusion and accepting and being tired and

[just drums]

Money Dance

look at them on friday—saturday night

                         before god come and clean them good

look the way their face sweating

               so that when you press that note on their forehead it

sticks for just a little while then shimmy

                 down—you never see nothing like it not anywhere

the way that palm wine fill them 'til their belly full

                     look at the money fall look at the way it falls

like problems falling away look at the way

                         they dance like problems falling away

look

If I Could Travel to Any Place and Any Time I Would

go to bed   with all the strangers who got my name right and party
like it was 1999 or 5pm somewhere in the empire

    i would drink jesus dry
watch me i would   ask for the most expensive stuff
i've already asked for so many things so i probably wouldn't have asked

if everybody started breaking stuff
    probably would have just broken stuff   as well
would have made sure that i got a big new telly

    during the riots
a man on the news is heard saying free nelson mandela   innit
    and i bet that he would   climb the prison gates himself

i bet he would try   love winnie himself
kiss babies sing freedom and happy i bet that he would

Watershed

    we were told
    to stay off the music channels
    but when michael sang ma makoosa
    we found ourselves fingering
    bass with mtv louded up
    soft carpet on toes headbanging
    with afros as close to the telly as possible
    went looking for cds our parents kept
    in cabinets
    found them

Ineffable Name

preacherman gave you your name. see, first he

made you wait several days for the sweat-

ed tongues and pidgin song to cease. o how

he teased payment for each syllable. o

how your mama she done spun straw into

gold for that name and

                                      now you tell me how

you gon' sell that name to the playground for

some cunt some tenderness. say boy, how you

sell your name and you don't know what it cost.

how you gon' let me find it in a box

full of trinkets beside the nose of an

egyptian and the picture of a man

you don't know no more cos he had your name

but sold it too, then ran. like traitors do.

Holy Roller

by rhythm by fire by force i'm sure
we moved wicked everything licking

    hungry

    sure we tasted something like umami
in the heat of it

how we wined we maybe whined
to it to sing a thing too honest too unruly
maybe singed

    when the day of pentecost come

we were one accord
one place   of this i'm sure

    it was a sunday
but of course   outside was a cold

that we mocked and that mocked
in turn   an ocean

on a bucket list that pagans swam in

i believing foolish in the heat of it
assumed sweat was communion
    fever god given

music   an undressing

the backdrop to a tonguing   and spirit
and spirit gave utterance and

spirit on all flesh
    and we were all filled
and we were

well done holy
    darkened swarthy bitter

as moon into blood become night

say darkening needed

    say we got the whine wrong
    forgot what we was whining for

We

living lavish
easy talking 'bout
baby this
baby that
like let me be
your baby-
lon talking
nothing but want

in every song
singing
my own name
talking nothing
but nothing but

JOHN 19:28

pour me water   please   pour some

    water   on me   i've been thirsting   for everyone

pour me   by the pint   pour me out

       o pour me silly   i've been talking awful fallow

   skin too ashy   tongue dry   pour me

something sweet   pour me sick   pour me

       on me

   i've been   thirsting for everything   pour me

     by the gallon   pour me stupid

           i've been thirsting something

of me   please   everything   on me   i've been talking

        awful   idle

i've been trifling   pour me

       fat   pour me empty

Confessions in 3/4 Timing

i stole wine and toiletries now the newspapers
have my face and i've been making playlists for crimes
that i haven't committed yet just so that i'll
be ready for it all like   *just murdered a man*
playlist   *robbed a bank now driving off cool* playlist
wrong place wrong time but he was no angel playlist

i ate pork and fat and shellfish and consumed blood
and blasphemed and mixed fabrics and broke the sabbath
and sold my name for silver coins and i boasted
i lied and i burnt down the family church and

    i beg   while i yet live let me do dumb shit still

i told you i wanted my mother's tribal mark
tattooed onto my stomach so it'd be like i
birthed my own africa whose lines i'd drawn myself
but all that i want is to brand and be branded

    i beg

i caught myself writing in okra and i found
that the words stink of each other   i caught myself
dancing that misery jazzed to rhythm and blues
    all dancing shoes and mouth giddy singing empty
all niggardly-hued and not quite it just right now
    now now now now now now now now just right now

Songs in the Key of Terror

    in this i am
        man most living
   most alive
      i know i

   so petite mort
        so rumpunchblooded
   so in the flesh
      of it i know so

   say me marvin
      paint me different
   shades of sunday
      holysomething

   i beg you promise
      to take
   me still
      still something

   take my throat
      still wet
   before time
      and folly make me all

o my
    days
you tar
    me so

end me early
    as it need
still wise before base
    i become

come on now

Swimming

and so over ocean
hoping we go
weathered by a toneless
sky grey /
mulatto. i let my spine
be your deck and i stroke.
the clothes from my back /
your flag. you stand
pointing new world i stroke
listen to you promising
ocean good blue.
i stroke i stroke slow
you promise stone into bread
water from stone
into water we go
your voice it goes on
but there's water in throat
and there's water
i stroke and there's water
we're drowning and i
as a boy could not swim
still i stroke. your voice
now a nothing
the water it sings
and we're drowning
i stroke

Notes

'OBIT.' is written after César Vallejo's 'Black Stone on a White Stone'.

'I' appropriates the language of Enoch Powell's 'Rivers of blood' speech delivered to a Conservative Association meeting in Birmingham on 20 April 1968.

Acknowledgements

Thanks are due to the editors of *Adjacent Pineapple*, *Alba*, *Ambit*, *Brittle Paper*, *Haverthorn* and *Ink Sweat & Tears*, in which some of these poems (or versions of them) have previously appeared.

Other titles by Bad Betty Press

Solomon's World
Jake Wild Hall

Unremember
Joel Auterson

In My Arms
Setareh Ebrahimi

The Story Is
Kate B Hall

The Dizziness Of Freedom
Edited by Amy Acre
and Jake Wild Hall

I'm Shocked
Iris Colomb

Ode to Laura Smith
Aischa Daughtery

The Pale Fox
Katie Metcalfe

TIGER
Rebecca Tamás

The Death of a Clown
Tom Bland

Milton Keynes UK
Ingram Content Group UK Ltd.
UKHW041406110923
428463UK00004B/245